The Commission

The Commission

The God Who Calls Us to Be a Voice during a Pandemic, Wildfires, and Racial Violence

Edited by
JEANNE C. DEFAZIO

Foreword by
JULIA C. DAVIS

Afterword by
MARTHA REYES

WIPF & STOCK · Eugene, Oregon

THE COMMISSION
The God Who Calls Us to Be a Voice during a Pandemic, Wildfires, and Racial Violence

Copyright © 2021 Jeanne C. DeFazio. All rights reserved. Except for brief quotations in critical publications or reviews, no part of this book may be reproduced in any manner without prior written permission from the publisher. Write: Permissions, Wipf and Stock Publishers, 199 W. 8th Ave., Suite 3, Eugene, OR 97401.

Wipf & Stock
An Imprint of Wipf and Stock Publishers
199 W. 8th Ave., Suite 3
Eugene, OR 97401

www.wipfandstock.com

PAPERBACK ISBN: 978-1-7252-8951-2
HARDCOVER ISBN: 978-1-7252-8950-5
EBOOK ISBN: 978-1-7252-8947-5

02/12/21

This book is dedicated to my beloved cousin Raquel
Fernandez who contracted the coronavirus
in a nursing home in 2020 and died.

Jeanne DeFazio

By The Same Authors

Julia C. Davis

Empowering English Language Learners, contributing author.
Keeping the Dream Alive: A Reflection on the Art of Harriet Lorence Nesbitt contributing author.
Specialist Fourth Class John Joseph DeFazio: Advocating For Disabled American Veterans, contributing author.
An Artistic Tribute to Harriet Tubman, author.

Jeanne C. DeFazio

Creative Ways to Build Christian Community (ed. with John P. Lathrop)
How to Have an Attitude of Gratitude on the Night Shift (with Teresa Flowers)
Redeeming the Screens (ed. with William David Spencer)
Berkeley Street Theatre: How Improvisation and Street Theater Emerged as Christian Outreach to the Culture of the Time (editor)
Empowering English Language Learners (ed. with William David Spencer)
Keeping the Dream Alive: A Reflection on the Art of Harriet Lorence Nesbitt (author and editor)
Specialist Fourth Class John Joseph DeFazio: Advocating For Disabled American Veterans, (editor)
Christian Egalitarian Leadership (contributing author).
An Artistic Tribute to Harriet Tubman, editor.

Martha Reyes

Keeping the Dream Alive: A Reflection on the Art of Harriet Lorence Nesbitt (contributing author)
Specialist Fourth Class John Joseph DeFazio: Advocating For Disabled American Veterans, contributing author.
Redeeming the Screens (contributing author)
Jesús y la Mujer Herida (Jesus and the Wounded Woman) (author)
Jesucristo, Tu Psicólogo Personal (Jesus Is Your Own Personal Psy-chologist) (author)
Por Que No Soy Feliz (Why Am I Not Happy?) (author)
Quiero Hijos Sanos (I Want Wholesome Children) (author)

Contents

Acknowledgements | ix
Foreword by Julia C. Davis | xi

Speak Up For Those Who Cannot Speak Up For Themselves | 1

SECTION ONE
Those who have contracted the corona virus and those who lost loved ones to the pandemic reached out to help others | 9

SECTION TWO
Those who are experiencing hardship are expressing it to identify with those who are suffering in the same way | 13

SECTION THREE
Those who have bonded with brothers and sisters in the community reflecting on shared experiences | 25

SECTION FOUR
Words of encouragement from ministers to comfort and reassure us | 41

Afterword by Martha Reyes | 53
About the Authors | 57
Bibliography | 59

Acknowledgements

EDITING THIS BOOK HAS been my privilege and honor. I want to thank Bruce I. McDaniel for reading the manuscript and making helpful suggestions. Thanks to Caleb Loring III for supporting this work. My sister Michelle DeFazio for working with the homeless sheltered in the San Diego Convention Center during the pandemic. My niece Ella Ryan for her great faith and resilience facing the challenges of the coronavirus lockdown. I am indebted to Peter Lynch for his kindness. Most of all I thank Jesus for giving me the strength to carry on.

Jeanne DeFazio

Foreword

Julia C. Davis

As a veteran teacher, it is my experience that we learn best from one another. This is termed 'peer learning' in the academic world:

> Peer learning should be mutually beneficial and involve the sharing of knowledge, ideas and experience between the participants. It can be described as a way of moving beyond independent to interdependent or mutual learning.[1]

I am contributing to this dialogue as an African American because I see the potential in it to bridge the racial divide. I have experienced both overt and covert racial prejudice in my lifetime. My scriptural and Constitutional convictions enable me to persevere and overcome. I believe that God *hath made of one blood all nations of men to dwell on all the face of the earth* (Acts 17:26). I swear allegiance to the Constitutional precept .. *that all men are created equal and endowed by their Creator with certain inalienable rights that among these are life, liberty and the pursuit of happiness.*[2]

In over thirty years teaching racially diverse inner city students, I applied these scriptural and constitutional principles developing strategies that empowered students to mobilize and

---

1. David Boud, "What is Peer Learning and Why is It Important?" lines 7–9, accessed 9/9/20.

2 "Life, Liberty and the Pursuit of Happiness." Lines 29–32, Accessed July 16, 2020.

succeed in predominantly white institutions of higher education. So many of these students have acquired professional status and make a difference in their own lives and within their communities. Structural racism prevents too many African Americans from reaching their God given potential:

> *Structural Racism in the U.S. is the normalization and legitimization of an array of dynamics – historical, cultural, institutional and interpersonal – that routinely advantage whites while producing cumulative and chronic adverse outcomes for people of color.* [3]

> *I've seen a lot of that and I know a lot of that to be true. It's not something you're meant to talk about in public, but it's something I'm talking about in public because that is very true.* [4] Jay Rockefeller

In the midst of the pandemic and shortly after the onset of the racial violence following the death of George Floyd,[5] my husband and I traveled from Massachusetts to California. We got a call from a California hospital regarding my husband's only and elder sister. She needed our help. Covid 19, violent protests, heightened dissatisfaction to the status quo were backdrops to travel to bring her from the West Coast to the East Coast. With determined resolve, my husband and I become intrepid travelers and overcomers on our return with his sister who needed twenty four hour care. I never anticipated riveting Fourth of July memories such as materialized during this year of fear. We were actually confronted by four police cars, two of which were unmarked, at the airport shuttle

---

3. Kenneth Laurence and Terry Keleher, "Structural Racism" lines 2–5, Accessed 9/18/20.

4 Everett, "Senators Duel Over Race Card," Lines 29–31, accessed June 29, 2020.

5 *On Memorial Day, May 25, 2020,* (an African American) *George Floyd died during his arrest for potentially stealing a pack of cigarettes. As a result, protests and riots have been occurring throughout the United States. While Floyd was being arrested, the arrest process was filmed not only by the store camera but by bystanders.* Spencers, "Responding to Floyd Killing," Lines 10–13. Accessed June 14, 2020.

terminal. God's favor, mercy and grace was profoundly prevalent in what could have easily escalated into a dangerous life threatening situation but instead the potentially arresting officer became a protective minister of God's divine intervention. The police officers actually pointed out and made a passage for us to the cell phone parking lot to sleep in our rental car until the airport shuttle bus came in the wee hours of the morning. One officer offered to watch over us to make sure no one would bother us until it was time to get the shuttle to the airport terminal. There were so many God-inspired episodes to retrieving my sister-in-law, that a whole chapter might not be sufficient to tell of God's delivering power. We traveled with her back to Massachusetts and spent the last few months moving her first to hospital care and a nursing home in the Boston area. She has been treated very well by the medical staff at Massachusetts General Hospital and she is now living in community with family. So many of my black brothers and sisters have not been as fortunate. Brother Curtis Almquist, SSJE explains:

> "Normal will never return, I hope not." An African American friend said this to me recently. She was speaking about the experience of injustice and suffering that has been so poignantly exposed during the coronavirus pandemic: the strains and inequities in healthcare, the economic disparity, the hijacking of hope and trust, the infectious cynicism, the display of racism. We have right now the opportunity to make changes in how we live and share life together. How shall we begin?[6]

I have had the opportunity to minister with Yvonnette O'Neal, Founder of Ambassadors Network Ministry. Yvonnette models racial equity for her community:

> African American church leader, Yvonnette O'Neal, founder of My Child Ministry, attended the memorial celebration of the fiftieth anniversary of Dr. King's March on the Washington D.C. Mall and commented favorably on the strong feeling of goodwill that prevailed among brothers and sisters of every color who attended. Ms. O'Neal

---

6. Curtis Almquist, "Making Meaning," 10.

Foreword

> explained that Dr. King was a pastor who understood that each Christian serves God by bringing souls to Jesus and that his civil rights activism sprang from his devotion to prayer and his obedience to God's word.[7]
>
> As an African American child, at the height of the civil rights movement in Mississippi, Yvonne was integrated into all-white schools. This experience taught her to relate to the individual, independent of race, color, or creed. In Southeast Washington, DC, as a young adult on staff at the Frederick Douglass Center and the Fishing School, her ethnic background gave her the education and social skills necessary to teach the predominately African American inner-city students how to develop in order to succeed in a multicultural society.[8] Through overcoming the challenges of her background, Yvonne has developed the ability to reach out in a multicultural church. She has ministered to mayors and members of Congress and city councils. Yvonnette expounds God's word by organizing all night Gospel Praise-a-Thons at the Lincoln Memorial, Prayer events of Christian leaders from across the nation at historic churches in the D.C. Metro Area and at Wailing Women International Intercessory Prayer events in key locations in the nation's capital. Her civil rights background and the profound influence of Dr. King have influenced her latest initiative to institute Bible Clubs as electives in the U.S. public school systems.[9]

At Yvonnette's request, I am highlighting the need for support within the South East D.C. community. The PBS Frontline Special, "During the pandemic, D.C. volunteers provide food for the needy" describes the plight of SouthEast Washington D.C. an area termed as 'across the river' because of a common local racial code.

---

7. Jeanne DeFazio, "We Shall Overcome." No longer available to access on Spencer's post.

8. DeFazio and Lathrop, *Creative Ways*, 24.

9. Jeanne DeFazio, "The Multicultural Aspect of Egalitarian Leadership," Spencer's, *Christian Egalitarian Leadership*, 118–119.

Foreword

> The area was already a notorious food desert, with one full-service grocery store for approximately 70,000 residents. And all manner of health issues strike disproportionately among its residents. Workers were some of the earliest victims of the economic shutdowns, and the closure of schools had an indirect effect on the basic nutrition of many students. "From asthma to high blood pressure, diabetes, you name it, we have it," said Ward 8 Councilman Trayon White. "And we have some of the highest food insecurities in this community." For those who were already poor and underserved, the impact of the coronavirus lockdown has been immediate and catastrophic. Low-wage hourly workers were some of the earliest victims of the economic shutdowns, and the closure of schools had an indirect effect on the basic nutrition of many students.[10]

These statistics impacted me greatly. I pray and do all I can to help others because Jesus, in John 21:15–17, commands: *If you love me, feed my sheep* and in Matthew 25:40 declares: *Truly I tell you, whatever you did for one of the least of these brothers and sisters of mine, you did for me.* We are all challenged by the pandemic, but we cannot forget our suffering brothers and sisters.

If you need help, contact me. I will help you if I can. Email: jdavis.ema@gmail.com.

---

10. Ashraf Khalil, "During pandemic, D.C. volunteers provide food for the needy," PBS, April 9, 2020, Accessed 9/17/20, lines 40–52.

Speak Up For Those Who Cannot Speak Up For Themselves

Introduction: Empathising with those who are suffering.

2020 HAS BEEN A season of tremendous challenge. Brother Lucas Hall describes it best:

> The United States right now is a country ravaged by two sicknesses, a global pandemic and the violence of racism. Both simultaneously demand a response and seem to swallow up anything most ordinary people are capable of doing, to render our best intentions and actions impotent in the face of these deadly plagues . . . So the question arises, when we feel paralyzed, when we feel impotent, when we feel stuck, what is God's call to us? . . . God's call is not something we plan for the future, but what we do right now in this and every moment. God's call does not cease.[1]

Everyone is called to belong to Christ and to participate in his creative and redemptive work.

Brother Curtis Almquist, SSJE, expressed the innate need for each person to make a difference:

> All of us are missionaries with a distinct set of gifts and abilities, with unique accesses to specific people and places. The fact that God has extended your life into this day is a

---

1. Lucas Hall, SSJE, "What is God's Call?" 5.

> sign of your vocation, your calling, that God has for you a mission that only you can fulfill.[2]

This writing project has become a platform for contributing authors from all walks of life who understand that during a pandemic, wildfires and racial violence, God is specifically calling them to speak up for those who cannot speak for themselves. Proverbs 31:8–9 gives the command: *Speak up for those who cannot speak for themselves, for the rights of all who are destitute. Speak up and judge fairly; defend the rights of the poor and needy.* These authors are all excellent communicators using the art form of writing as a platform for individual and collective well being:

> Access to arts opportunities and participation in the arts can dramatically improve health outcomes and well-being, counter inequalities and increase social engagement. As a supplement to medicine and care, the evidence suggests that engagement with the arts can improve a person's physical and mental well-being. The benefits of arts activities are being seen beyond traditional settings, and their role in supporting communities and individuals who would otherwise be excluded is increasingly being recognized.[3]

In the Old Testament, God called the prophets to bring His word home to his people (Ezekiel 33:1–9). As members of the New Covenant of Grace, Christians are all called to prophetic work (Acts 2:33).

Aída Besançon Spencer

> What can Christians say from a biblical perspective about the current coronavirus pandemic? Some have cited 2 Chronicles 7:13–15 and called for a season of humbling oneself and seeking God's face. 2 Chronicles 7:13–15 contains God's guidance to King Solomon after the temple is dedicated. He speaks to a man who begins strong as a believer but, then, in his later years, will fall apart. Solomon

---

2. Curtis Almquist, SSJE, "Making Meaning," 11.
3. "Arts Health and Well Being," 1.

is a model for the nation. God warns Solomon that when Solomon and the nation of Israel sin, their sin results in punishments such as drought, locusts, or pestilence that can be ended if the people "humble themselves, pray, seek [God's] face, and turn from their wicked ways." The nation will be warned ahead of time (e.g., 1 Kings 11). But, is that exactly the situation now? Is God punishing the whole world for its sins? . . .

[No, instead, Jesus recommended two actions in Luke 13:1-4]: 1. Prepare for your own death because it can occur at any moment. Are you ready to meet your Maker and Judge (Luke 13:3, 5)? 2. Prepare for this forthcoming disaster by helping those affected (Acts 11:29–30).[4] . . . Prayer and seeking God's face are the right moves at this time, but let's do it all together so that we can be a model to the world of God's loving kindness and community compassion . . . 1. We can pray to the God who created us and loves us and wants the best for us. 2. We can be calm because we have no illusions that we are going to live on this old earth forever. God can protect us until our time to be with him has come. 3. We are not alone. Find a church family that cares for you and can pray for you and hold you up. 4. We need to remember that we do not get sick by being with people. We get sick by being around sick people, so we do not have to fear everyone. If we are calm, we can use our God-given common sense and also be generous with others. 5. Remember the reasons that you may have to thank God in the midst of this terrible time . . . Two additional Bible passages come to our mind: Philippians: 4:6: "Do not worry about anything, but in everything by prayer and supplication with thanksgiving let your requests be made known to God" and Proverbs 6:6: "Go to the ant, you lazybones, consider its ways, and be wise." These two passages balance each other: rely on God, but God also responds most to a praying believer who then acts with consideration for others.[5]

---

4. Please read our book *Joy through the Night: Biblical Resources on Suffering* (Wipf and Stock) on the four basic reasons for suffering. This pandemic fits under a "world of pain."

5. Aída and Bill Spencer, "Who's Fault is the Virus?" Accessed September

The Commission

Aida Spencer, A New Testament professor.

The call on our lives in a crisis is to speak up. California is besieged by the coronavirus pandemic and the worst wildfires in its history. In his September 14, 2020, *New York Times* interview, Jerry Brown, the former governor of California, describes how he could barely make out the mountains in the distance from his ranch in the city of Williams:

> *He never thought the air around his home, which he built in the wilderness of his family ranch, an hour's drive north of Sacramento, would be this shrouded.... (While he maintained that climate change is a major cause of the wildfires) Mr. Brown acknowledged that the devastating fires were partly the result of the failure of the state and the federal government to thin forests, which are now filled with trees that died in the drought — fuel for the fires.... he said that ingrained policies in states like California, with its sprawl, devotion to single-family houses and reliance on automobiles, had also contributed to the crisis.*[6]

The call on our lives in human tragedy is to empathize with those who suffer as we have suffered. In the summer of 2020, digital images of California's towering infernos, evacuees, firefighters and ravaged homes have saturated news outlets and social media. My uncle, a Butte County, California psychiatrist, kindly contributed this account of his evacuation from the Camp Fires in 2018. At his request, I am publishing it anonymously. It resonates with the life and death experiences of so many wildfire victims during the pandemic:

> *The most destructive and deadliest fire in the history of California began at 6:29 A.M. on Thursday, November 8, 2018 near the intersection of Pulga and Camp Creek roads, which is near Highway 70 and the north fork of the Feather River about 10 miles northeast of Paradise. About that same time, PG&E learned that it was having problems*

14, 2020.

6. Nagourney, Adam,"Jerry Brown on a California Exodus, Tell Me Where Are We To Go?" accessed September 15, 2020, lines 1-7, 16-29, 115-130.

with its power lines. The fire destroyed 15,580 structures – 11,990 of which were homes. One of those homes was the family home on Ryan Road. Another was the home of my son and his family on Neal Road. Nearly four months later, on March 11, 2019, according to a front page article in the Sacramento Bee, PG&E admitted that a broken hook "probably" caused the fire by allowing a wire from a 115-kilowatt transmission tower to make contact with the tower itself which showered the very dry ground below with sparks.

 These are descriptions of what we experienced that fateful day. At 7:55 A.M., our neighbor on Ryan Road called our house and told my wife– who was sleeping in the living room and picked up the phone – to wake me up because there was a fire. My wife came back to the bedroom and told me of the call. At 8:00 A.M., my son, who had arrived the evening before, was called by a high school friend who lives in Oregon. He said his brother who lived on lower Pentz Road in Paradise called to tell him he had received a phone call to evacuate because there was a fire nearby. I walked with our dog up our driveway to open the gate so we wouldn't be trapped. I had totally forgotten that the gate was operated by a battery and would have opened even if the power was cut off. Our neighbor was standing near the gate. He pointed out the intense orange glow in the entire eastern sky. There was a very loud sound like a number of leaf blowers all operating at once. When I asked our neighbor what it was, he said it was the wind generated by the fire. He said that he and his wife were about to leave and he advised me to do the same. I immediately went back home and grabbed some shopping bags out of one of our cars. By 8:15 A.M. I began putting our medications in the bags because I had heard that they were the first items to take when evacuating. There was an empty box in the front hall which, fortunately, I had delayed putting in the recycling container. In it, from my bedroom, I put the stock certificates and the red book containing the history of all the stock transactions (started by my parents in 1965). I grabbed my laptop and my checkbook from the table. I went back to the downstairs room to get from the safe the family rings, a portion of the coin collection which contained some gold coins and the "pink slips" for our three cars. My son grabbed the family Bible from downstairs and two of my grandmother's paintings. I yelled to him to also get the family trust. Once he got upstairs he began putting in a cardboard box all the family pictures which were hanging on the wall of the bedroom hall. In the rush we left behind many other family pictures.

By 8:45 A.M. we had received a phone call to evacuate and we were loading up my son's sedan and my 2001 Ford Escape with the boxes of belongings. My wife and our fifteen year old little dog, Angel, rode in my son's sedan. I drove the Escape. We left around 9:10 A.M. At the end of Ryan Road I stopped and ran back to my son's car to ask him where we were going. He replied we were going to my son and daughter-in-law's home on Neal Road because that area of town had not been told to evacuate. It was lucky that we turned left on Kibler Road to go to Nunneley Road because we later learned that had we turned right to go to Billie Road, cars there were not moving because of gridlock and flames were so close to the road that folks were leaving their cars and fleeing on foot. The first fire we encountered was rather small and was about half a mile from our house. My son called 911 to report it but was told there were fires all over town. My daughter-in-law and granddaughter had left to get us but were turned back at the intersection of Pearson and Clark. My daughter-in-law called my son and they agreed to meet at her house. However, when she got back to her house she decided they needed to evacuate.

At roughly 11:30 A.M. after driving through cars gridlocked on both lanes of Nunneley Road and Pearson Road we arrived at my son and daughter-in-law's house on Neal Road. The gates were open and we drove into the driveway and found they had already left. My son's car was low on gas and so he decided to leave it there and we moved everything into the Escape and started down Neal Road toward Highway 99 with my son driving. By 12:35 P.M. we finally arrived at Highway 99. It took nearly three and a half hours because Neal Road was clogged with cars and most of the time nothing moved. Flames were within twenty feet of both sides of the road all the way to the County dump.

Persons were abandoning their cars on the sides of the road and running in panic. Neal Road was reduced to one lane because the uphill lane was open only for emergency vehicles. The likelihood that we could be trapped inside our car by the fire was very real. In spite of my misgivings, my son took the opportunity of the open lane to pass a long line of cars. Fortunately, no emergency vehicles were coming up the hill. Traffic started to move when traffic on 99 was finally blocked which allowed cars on Neal Road to proceed without delay either north or south on Highway 99. We turned south to go toward Folsom.

Although much was lost in the fire that can never be replaced we were fortunate to have escaped alive and not physically hurt as was also the case for my son's family. Had our son not come the evening before to help his mother get to her dental appointment the next morning I doubt that we would have been so fortunate.[7]

---

7. Anonymous contributing author, interview by email, September 14, 2020.

Section One

Those who have contracted the corona virus and those who lost loved ones to the pandemic reached out to help others

Larry DeFazio

It all started in early April 2020 with a back ache. I work in an office setting and was feeling uncomfortable as I sat at my desk. By that time, one of my co-workers had already tested positive for COVID-19 but it was not a real cause for concern since I had not had any recent direct contact with him. In observance of protocol, I notified my supervisors and was sent home where I tried to isolate myself as much as possible from my wife and two adult sons. At that time, my wife's dental office had already closed down but both of my sons were still working, one as a logistics manager for a military contractor and the other as a medic with a private ambulance service. The next day, I was experiencing a slight headache and body aches so I went to a walk-in medical facility to be examined in anticipation of being tested for COVID-19. Pandemic protocols were in place so I was not allowed into the facility. It was still cold out so they had a problem obtaining an accurate body temp which was frustrating since their own protocols

> were hindering the entire process. After being seen at the walk-in medical facility, I was sent for COVID-19 testing at the county testing center. Due to my employment with the county, my testing was expedited and I was the first to be tested at this new drive-through facility. Of course, the result was positive and I was subsequently contacted by the county Health Department and advised of proper protocol. The end result was my being off work for three weeks during which I experienced mild flu-like symptoms including aches, a slight fever, occasional cough, and loss of appetite. At the time, I was fifty-two years of age, exercising regularly, and free of any preexisting conditions. It was not the worst bout of flu I had ever dealt with but it did take a toll as I lost about ten pounds and most of my strength since I could not exercise. It made me realize how someone with a preexisting health condition or someone of advanced age could be hit hard by this flu. During my period of sickness, my youngest son began to experience symptoms and also tested positive for COVID-19. As mentioned earlier, he was working with a private ambulance service and had been in several hospitals and convalescent facilities prior to any pandemic protocols being put in place. My theory is that he had been an asymptomatic carrier and that I contracted it from him. By the time it was all said and done, my wife and oldest son also began to experience mild flu-like symptoms and, although they were never tested, theorized that they had contracted COVID-19. Prior to returning to work at her dental office, my wife was tested for the antibodies and it was determined that they were present in her blood. Although the pandemic affected my planned travel to California in August and October of 2020, I am thankful that none of our friends or extended family had been affected up to this point.[1]

Larry DeFazio, married, physically active fifty-two year-old father of two with no preexisting health conditions.

---

1. Larry DeFazio, interview by email, September 22, 2020.

Speak Up For Those Who Cannot Speak Up For Themselves

Inez DeFazio

> My niece Raquel Fernandez contracted coronavirus in a nursing home and died on September 13, 2020. The grief my family felt at her passing was acute. I spent the same afternoon in the Emergency Room of Sutter Hospital in Davis, California. At ninety one, I naturally avoid going into an emergency room during a pandemic but it was Sunday and I needed to monitor my heart. The emergency room was filled with very sick people. The excellent medical staff checked me out quickly. My statistics, thank God, were all very good. As you probably know, those emergency room days can be a real cross. At my age when I walk into the emergency room I feel I may not walk out alive. When I walked out of the sliding glass door alive, I knew the Lord blessed me with another day and I thanked him with all my heart. My gratitude was profound. I breathed more easily. I pray for all those with COVID-19 in emergency rooms worldwide that God's loving presence and healing power touches their lives. In Jesus' Name, Amen. [2]

Inez DeFazio, co-founder of Yolo County Coalition Against Hunger.

Daniel J. Arnerich

In January 2020, Dan's mother died at the age of ninety-four of natural causes. Dan was her only child. They were very close and the transition during the pandemic has been a challenge. He has put aside his own grief and reached out to his Aunt Inez. She misses her sister and appreciates Dan's calls and FaceTime visits.

> In 2020, Jesus and the angels took my mother home to heaven. In the past year, so many families lost loved ones to COVID-19. My heart reaches out to them. I understood the pain and grief. It is sad that fear of contagion prevents them from being with their loved ones to say goodbye. It is painful to be unable to gather together to celebrate the lives of deceased loved ones. I have been going through grief

---

2. Inez DeFazio, interview in person, September 14, 2020.

myself and understand the sense of loss. Let's remember to pray for and reach out to those who cannot be with their family members who are sick and dying of COVID-19. God bless you all. [3]

Daniel J. Arnerich, Retiree, California State Capitol Secretary of State's Office.

---

3. Daniel J. Arnerich, interview by text, September 12, 2020.

Section Two

Those who are experiencing hardship are expressing it to identify with those who are suffering in the same way

Teresa "Two Feathers" Flowers

Before retiring and moving to Pine Bluff, Arkansas, Teresa became known as the "Mother Teresa" of Beverly, Massachusetts. She worked with at risk youth in the town's private and government programs. Her devotional, *How to Have An Attitude of Gratitude on the Night Shift,* is filled with prayers in poetry form that she prayed over the children during night shift supervision. "Lonely Night of the Soul" is part of this collection:

> "*Lonely Night of the Soul*"
> *When fears grip my thoughts, I come face to face with the children's pain, Their lonely night of the soul. Then the Lord's strength comes out from deep within me to battle the pain of their past with Love.*[1]

---

1. Flowers, *Attitude of Gratitude,* 6.

> I am retired and cannot afford to own and operate a car. Taking public transportation during the pandemic is risky. I have been walking to the store in good weather. Pine Bluff, Arkansas, where I reside, has had extreme weather patterns during the 2020 pandemic.
>
> Where could I go but to the Lord? During this pandemic I feel that God's hand is slowly being taken off the earth but His hand is still on His children's safety and protection. I know this from being able to run to shelter from a tornado. I know this from having to walk to the hospital and praying for God's traveling mercies when a sister in Christ stopped and gave me a ride, saying "God told her to." "Where could I go? Only to the Lord?" Every time I needed transportation, God came through. Praising the Lord for his mercy. Amen. I am living Lamentations 3:22–23: *The steadfast love of the Lord never ceases; his mercies never come to an end; they are new every morning; great is your faithfulness.*[2]

Teresa Flowers, author of *How to Have An Attitude of Gratitude on the Night Shift.*

Steve Boutry

> So, I'm a pastor. I'm supposed to guide people towards faith and mystery, an appreciation of things hidden and unseen. More specifically, I am to guide people in a life of prayer. A conversation with God. To be brutally honest, I had many ideas and concepts surrounding this task, but it became visceral and real in a very unsettling way on March 11, 2020. In no way do I mean to diminish the great suffering that this pandemic has caused, but for far too many Americans our comfortable existence has significantly eroded our ability to pray. Well, no more, at least for me. I have prayed from the guts for the past six months. Has it changed world history? Probably not. But it has indeed changed me, and sent me into the present and the future

---

2. Teresa Flowers, interview by text, September 12, 2020.

more reliant on God, on mystery, on power other than my own than ever before.³

Steve Boutry serves as Lead Pastor of Discovery Christian Church in Davis, California. Do Justice, Love Mercy, Walk Humbly, Live a Simple Life.

Jozy Pollock

I had gone through something similar to this pandemic when I was a child in London during World War Two. We had to have blackout curtains and couldn't open the door unless lights were out. If there was a chink of light showing the warden would be banging on the door. The gas masks were far more uncomfortable than the masks people are complaining about these days. In Great Britain people were all in one accord to fight the enemy and of course people weren't walking around carrying weapons that should only be used on a battlefield. It is horrifying to see so many Americans display attitudes of selfishness and self-entitlement in the midst of terrible human suffering. I do really feel sorry for those that suffer with depression. Women who are shut in with an abusive spouse and parents who have to be teachers too. God bless all the people who have put their lives on the line to serve those who haven't had the privilege of being able to stay home. There is so much tragedy going on right now with the fires and the storms where people have lost everything. My heart goes out to them and I keep praying for rain to help the courageous firefighters. I have adjusted well to isolation in the pandemic due to the fact that my car lease was up in November 2019 and for various reasons I chose to join the Lyft group. Needless to say after driving for over sixty years it was difficult. If I needed to go somewhere I had someone drive me. If I wanted to go somewhere I had to find someone who also wanted to go and most times I just stayed home. When the pandemic hit I was so used to staying home that it didn't make that much difference to me. I am blessed as I can be alone and never feel lonely. I have Jesus.

3. Steve Bounty, interview by email, October 1, 2020.

> I am born again. We all miss meeting up with friends and hugging each other but do we want to be a spreader and responsible for someone getting sick? I certainly don't. We are the church not some building and many who were disobedient to the law and the warnings died from the virus. In January 2020, I got very ill and was in the hospital so I especially don't want to risk infection. I confess I am almost embarrassed to admit to being a Christian due to my disappointment with the church at large. We are supposed to be a good example to the world but I am seeing quite the opposite behavior. The truth is that I have never been disappointed with Jesus. Accepting Jesus as my Lord and Savior brought me out of relationships in the Hollywood elite and brought me into a relationship with the God of the Universe. If you are feeling the effect of the pandemic, let Jesus into your heart. He will heal you and love you and guide you through it all with tender mercy and love. 2020 has made me more aware of how much we need God's mercy and Jesus' gift of reconciliation in the midst of acute human suffering. As the center of hope in a world gone awry, the promise of grace embodied the hope of reconciling humanity to the redeeming God, as he was given as God's gift to lead and inspire us all to do works of mercy and reconciliation.[4]

Jozy Pollock, author *Backstage Pass To Heaven.*

Louise Maguire

> The pandemic has most certainly affected my family by limiting both our time and involvement with each other. My brother and his family in Orange County are very reluctant to travel north to visit. This reluctance is highly attributed to the number of cases of coronavirus in a number of counties in the state of California, especially in the Central Valley. My brother has been stranded in the city of Oroville due to the North Complex Fire. He is also very reluctant to visit any family due to the contagious nature of

---

4. DeFazio, *Keeping the Dream Alive,* 27. Jozy Pollock, interview by email, September 17, 2020.

Speak Up For Those Who Cannot Speak Up For Themselves

> this virus. My parents have relocated from Paradise to Folsom since the Camp Fire completely destroyed our family home in Paradise. Due to the advanced age of both of my parents they are sequestered in Folsom. Although we visit them on a regular basis we must follow the guidelines of social distancing. Unfortunately due to this virus our visits are less frequent. I do visit my daughter and grandchildren frequently and also assist my granddaughter with distance learning. One of my granddaughters was born during the pandemic. We were unable to visit her at the hospital due to the pandemic. It was a very huge disappointment for me. Although she is now happy and healthy, I will forever regret not seeing my new granddaughter immediately after her birth.[5]

Louise Maguire, Psychiatric Social Worker.

Mary Ann DeFazio

These two entrees are excerpts from my journal

> Friday, May 29: The weather has been scorching hot these past three days but is beginning to cool today. What a relief. As a happy, early start to our day, Allie and I took a long, cool walk and scooter-ride around the neighborhood. We both enjoyed it. I'm worried that what once seemed impossible now seems quite routine. When I first imagined being IN quarantine for two, possibly three weeks, I could barely stand the thought. It now feels normal. Other than my walks around the neighborhood and the occasional lonely drive, It IS routine. That does not mean I'm happy about it. In fact, I've struggled with sadness and loneliness. It's difficult for all of us. Poor Allie is feeling caged. It's not normal for a girl, almost six, to stay away from the kids she loves to play with. Christina keeps her engaged with activities and school-time distance learning with her teacher. We also play! We have fun. We do baking, cooking and science projects, and make messes. But it's not the same. I feel sorry for her. Now, as Sacramento County Stay

---

5. Louise Maguire, interview by mail, September 16, 2020.

Home restrictions begin to loosen, I am not feeling any better. I predict that we will see a spike in infections and that means it's more dangerous for me to go anywhere. I want this to be over.

Monday, June 1: Last Monday, May 25, there was an act of violent restraint by a Minneapolis police officer on a man suspected of passing a counterfeit bill at a store. The man, who was held down by a knee on his neck for over eight minutes, while in handcuffs, was named George Floyd. Mr. Floyd died of apparent asphyxiation, there on the street, with three other officers watching. Since that day, now one week ago, there have been protests. Black Lives Matter! I have always believed this truth. Now, as the grandmother of a bi-racial child, it's personal. The protests were first in Minneapolis but have since spread to several other major cities and small towns all around the country. Sacramento is, tonight, in the midst of its fourth night of protest, or as they now have become, riots. Tonight, Sacramento has declared the city shut down, from 8:00 P.M. until 6:00 A.M. There has been growing violence and destruction and I believe there will be more tonight. Violence isn't the answer. It dilutes and bastardizes the meaning and dignity by which BLM operates. I believe that the damage is being done by people whose message hasn't been heard. It hasn't been heard for generations! There IS anger! I am angry. But violence isn't the answer! The message of Peaceful demonstration is being ignored. But violence is the wrong message. I pray that dignity will someday soon be afforded to all people of our country, especially those of us who have waited generations to be seen. I hear helicopters....[6]

Mary Ann DeFazio, retired Head Start teacher.

Mike Taesali

Mike Taesali is a Davis, California musician who has performed in many of the town's churches. His acts of kindness are legendary in his community.

---

6. Mary Ann DeFazio, interview by email, September 17, 2020.

> For years I worked as a crosswalk guard for the Davis Unified School District. Last year, the school district stopped using the contractor that employed me. I was able to collect unemployment which ended as the pandemic began. I have my own hauling business in Davis. When students move in or out of housing, I get a lot of business. I applied for unemployment at the onset of the pandemic and after a few months qualified. Then the federal government shutdown unemployment payments in July of 2020. In September, I just received notification that I am eligible to apply again for unemployment. I thank God for that. Also for the fact that my family is well. I feel God is drawing me closer to him during the hardships of this pandemic. Nahum 1:7 reminds me, "The LORD is good, a strong refuge when trouble comes. He is close to those who trust in him." Trust in the Lord, He will come through for you![7]

Mike Taesali, musician and prayer warrior.

Matt DeFazio

> Thankfully, my family has not suffered directly as a result of the COVID-19. To date, we are all still relatively healthy, employed and enjoying life, albeit somewhat quieter and less active given the many business closures. That said, we were all very concerned our respective places of employment may get shut down, and we are very sorry for those unable to continue in their work. After six months of closures, we are still perplexed by the interpretation of "essential worker." Though grateful for my family's good health (still enjoying one another on a regular basis) and our uninterrupted employment, I am very concerned about a Sacramento icon that is a significant part of my life these days. Fairytale Town, for which I am a board member, is struggling to remain financially viable. Though it has provided immeasurable joy for literally millions of children (250,000 visitors/year), countless family memories and endless learning opportunities for over sixty-one years, it is having a difficult time getting visitors to return in numbers

---

7. Mike Taesali, interview by text, September 13, 2020.

necessary to keep the doors open. The hard-working, efficient, and above all, wonderful staff continues to do everything they can to convey to the community that the park is open for business, but would-be visitors have shared concerns over the mask requirements and the potential spread of the virus, discouraging them from enjoying the park. As understandable as that is, those concerns can be effectively resolved by adhering to the prudent safety measures posted on prominent signs throughout the park, as well as on the Fairytale Town website. In due time, we'll see how this story plays out, but for now, we will continue to hope for the best for Fairytale Town . . . and all regional businesses, large and small, iconic and mundane, woven into the fabric of our unique and tight-knit community.[8]

Matt DeFazio is a middle-aged forever-resident of Sacramento, a husband to his high school sweetheart, father of three wonderful sons and a member of a large, happy Italian-American family.

Billie Hemphill

At the onset of the lockdown my ex-husband, who works in the medical field, was furloughed. He applied for unemployment but never received it. If he had not been put back on the job recently, I would have lost my home. In Oregon, where I reside, five hundred thousand people have been forced to evacuate their homes because of wildfires. The smoke index in Oregon is off the chart and is at a dangerous level. I have had to prepare to evacuate at a moment's notice. In the meantime I have covered the windows to keep the smoke levels down. There has been a great loss of lives and property. The California/Oregon border was closed because the smoke along Interstate five was so dense you couldn't see to drive safely. Phoenix and Talent, Oregon burned to the ground. In the prisons near Portland inmates are experiencing respiratory problems because of the toxic air quality. What has held me together in this challenging time is my strong faith in God. He is answering my prayers and has put his hand of protection over me.

8. Matt DeFazio, interview by email. September 29, 2020.

Speak Up For Those Who Cannot Speak Up For Themselves

I want to encourage anyone who is experiencing all that I just described to pray and ask God for help and direction. He will answer those prayers. You are not alone. I am praying for you.[9]

Billie Hemphill, historian/genealogist.

Gladys Inzofu

I have worked in terrifying circumstances like war zones where I experienced bombs, bomb-shelling, evacuations, but I have never been scared like I was with COVID-19. It was not the virus itself that was scary but the processes involved. As a health care worker I have dealt with arrays of disease outbreaks and the process brought calmness and helped to alleviate fear both to health workers and patients in order to execute appropriate processes and bring control to the outbreak. The despair I saw both in my patients and my colleagues was so overwhelming and a hindrance to look ahead for a believer like me. It is at this time that I realize the true fear that the enemy can bring unto people and through fear those people can die without realization. I came to understand that fear led me to stay in my mask for all the hours I worked. I did not drink or eat anything for a period of 8–16 hours. I was tired, dizzy, and weak every day but still woke up to go to work to look at the frail faces of my patients and give them hope. The impact came later when I was not able to go to work because of fatigue and the thought that I had contracted the virus yet it was all fear. Above all, when you look at your patients and see them seeking hope in you, looking directly into your eyes asking, "will I make it?" With their eyes glued on the TV sets translating information into their situations, it was so devastating. At the end ensuring somebody of living and ending up losing them was terrifying and impacted greatly on my faith. I left a few to the Lord and encouraged them everyday to look at the Cross of Jesus but many did not want to hear that. Those I led to the Lord survived and they were happy when they tested negative. Some of my

---

9. Billie Hemphill, interview by email, September 14, 2020.

> colleagues blamed God: why did He allow COVID-19 to attack? I found myself at the defense of God: it is our own sins in the land that has led to all these tragedies as in the days of the Israelites in the wilderness led by Moses. I thank God for He is gracious even with all that we have gone through, many still remember God in the process and yet many have forgotten God who is precious to call upon at the time of crisis, now He is no longer God when the new norm seems normal. Is it going to be the new normal?[10]

Gladys Inzofu, RN, MA SID, DNP in progress.

Mary Ciarcia

> Thank you for asking me to contribute. This touches me a lot. During the pandemic, the Lord called me into deep prayer. The result of all this prayer was that He healed painful memories that had haunted me for years. He took the burden I had had away from me and gave me a peace and freedom I had never known. Since then, He's been teaching me to rest in Him. I am so grateful, praise Him, and give Him all the glory. So much of what He did was in the subconscious, so it's really hard to explain. God bless you.[11]

Mary Ciarcia, International English as a Second Language Teacher.

Lori Croup Chang

> The pandemic and the California wildfires have kept me inside my house. I have wanted to limit my exposure to both. These events have forced me to slow down. Anything and everything becomes a meditation, an exercise in mindfulness—preparing a meal, sorting and doing laundry, making the bed. Taking long, deep breaths and even engaging my heart and mind in prayer helps me relax and realize these crises will pass and better days are

---

10. Gladys Inzofu, interview by email, September 30, 2020.
11. Mary Ciarcia, interview by email, September 10, 2020.

> ahead of us. I was holding my breath a lot! It took me a while to develop self-awareness. The deep, slow breathing is what helps with anxiety. Many people experience anxiety because they are holding their breath or breathing quick, shallow breaths. I have a funny story on that one . . . I used to feel annoyed that in therapy they focused so much on breath. I kept thinking, "Really?!? We're talking about breathing AGAIN?" It really is like a reset for our body and also carries oxygen to all our cells. Racism. It's a tough one. What I've been doing is trying to initiate conversations with my African American friends, hear their particular concerns, and then mostly listen. I feel that my white privilege shields me from racism. However, I am in a biracial marriage which draws some prejudiced thoughts and comments from others. I try to respond with kindness outwardly even if it causes me to feel anger. In the words of Martin Luther King Jr., ". . . I have a dream that one day this nation will rise up and live out the true meaning of its creed: 'We hold these truths to be self-evident, that all men are created equal.'"[12] I 'm glad for my faith in God. I can tell Him what upsets and saddens me and know He understands.[13]

Lori Croup Chang is a pastor's wife and the mother of three adult children who enjoys gardening, novels, theater and films.

Sheri Pedigo

> The impact of the pandemic encouraged me to leave my home in California to move closer to my family 3,000 miles away. It was very challenging moving across the country as things were very volatile not knowing if I was going to be able to drive into the next state. As a result most of my performances were canceled so there was no real need for me to stay in California. I don't particularly like working from home but I had to reinvent myself and start teaching online courses of songwriting and vocal instruction. I

---

12 "Martin Luther King, Jr.,"I Have A Dream" Speech, Accessed September 12, 2020.

13 Lori Croup Chang, interview by email, September 10, 2020.

have downsized quite a bit and decluttered my life. Half the things we hold onto we don't even need. Most of the time we don't have the time to go through them to get rid of them. It rains a lot in the South, not like the sunny outdoors of California so being inside has not been as bad as it would've been if I stayed in California with the sun shining beautifully outside. I have utilized and been very productive with my time. I've even taken the time to sell a lot of my items that I don't need to make some extra income. We are adaptable creatures; we learn to adapt. Scripture has sustained me. I believe that God can turn all things together for the good no matter what the circumstance. I call God into remembrance of the promise of His Word daily: And we know that all things work together for good to those that love God, to those who are called according to his purpose. Romans 8:28.[14]

Sheri Pedigo, Grammy Award nominated lyricist.

---

14. Sheri Pedigo, interview by text, September 14, 2020.

Section Three

Those who have bonded with brothers and sisters in the community reflecting on shared experiences

Donna Thayer

Donna Louise Thayer is a dedicated educator who cares deeply about the lives of her students. She contributed to this dialogue in the midst of adapting her school to the COVID-19 reality.

> Life has taught me that much is learned about grace, wisdom and character only when seen through the rearview mirror. Both joy and loss are amplified in their permanence. These last several months have indeed provided lessons in both the fragility and the strength of everyday life in the form of seemingly insignificant occurrences that, until they are gone, can be so easily taken for granted. The coronavirus pandemic, with its accompanying real and imagined loss, has provided such lessons. The resulting and continuing heartbreaking loss of life, of livelihoods, and of economic and physical well-being has forever altered what I take for granted. I have been fortunate to have been able to work from home, to maintain my career and even to enjoy daily life once again. Yet, the images of loss, suffering

and despair caused by 2020's coronavirus pandemic are never far from my mind.[1]

Donna Thayer, M Ed, Vice Principal

Gemma Wenger

My COVID-19 Experience. As an assistant principal, I stood in the front office of my elementary school site when I first heard the announcement that schools would be closing. My first emotion was actually happiness followed by uncertainty about the future. I was overworked and needed a break. The idea of staying home really sounded like an opportunity to lighten my load and get other pressing matters for my ministry and personal life completed. It was exactly that. While the school district figured out how to service children remotely, I made great use of my time. My church meetings were held via Facebook Live and then, when small gatherings were permitted, reconvened in person. The work of the Lord must never stop! I continued to produce and edit my television shows "Beauty for Ashes" and "Gemma Wenger's Hollywood" as well as record my radio show "Heart of God Radio" at Salem Broadcasting Studios for KKLA and KPRZ. While others ran reruns and stayed home, I showed up to provide new material for listeners who needed encouragement and support during this difficult season. I never stopped working. I used the opportunity for a traffic-less freeway to go where I needed to go in less than a fourth of the time. I walked my dog up and down my street and met my neighbors who would have been in the gym or on a hiking trail had they not closed. I took the opportunity to run up and down my two long flights of stairs traversing my hillside and care for my orchard that was badly in need of attention. Once the school district informed me that Zoom meetings and distance learning from home would be the new protocol, I rejoiced when I figured out the time I would have used to drive to work could now be better spent cleaning my house, running errands, watering my garden, getting a few

---

1. Donna Louise Thayer, interview by email, September 12, 2020.

extra winks of sleep, or playing with my new Bichon Frise puppy. The unnecessary focus and inordinate amount of time finding the perfect outfit and putting on make-up decreased significantly as I threw on a decent top and some jeans that would never be seen by my computer camera utilized by Zoom. My morning workout classes, once held in Palisades Park overlooking the ocean, were now held in my living room via Zoom. I didn't have to get up as early to get to them, and afterward I could run into the next room to take a quick shower before I landed in front of my computer in the dining room for my early 9:00 A.M. meeting just in the nick of time. My Zoom skills increased tremendously. People were amazed in my workout class when I was able to put up a reaction such as a thumbs up or clapping emoji. I held Individualized Education Program (IEP) meetings via Zoom and learned how to hand over my computer remotely to the participants to sign in. I became Future Ready Certified when I took a Webinar with over 16,000 participants that I could not see. I was really enjoying the changes it made in my work schedule, and the new opportunities it afforded me. When distance learning is no longer the classroom norm, I am going to continue using Zoom for meetings with parents and staff members. People are more likely to attend when they don't have to drive and can participate in the comfort of their own home.

Unfortunately, one of my tenants who was renting a single-family home that I owned near the marina was hit hard by the impact of COVID-19. They owned a limousine company which was affiliated with a company in New York and Florida. Because everything had closed down, the $20,000 check that they were owed never arrived, and thus my rent stopped coming. I had to float the mortgage payments on my own. I never stopped paying my mortgage even though the banks were willing to work with me, and I have not to this day. Additionally, one of my other tenants in a fourplex that I owned in Santa Monica moved out to seek cheaper housing in Orange County. After an extensive remodel, the effect of COVID-19 had caused many renters to move back home with their families and forego their independent lifestyle until the return of a more prosperous *economy. Hence my gorgeous high-end remodel sits vacant in need of a loving tenant. A couple that I had known for a long time had just returned from Iran and attended my prayer meeting. Everything was so new at the time that no one really understood quarantining. They ended up testing positive for COVID-19. I then called my doctor and because there were no tests available she let me know that the best thing to do was isolate for 14 days. I complied and put literally everything on hold for 14 days. I can't say I didn't enjoy it. Resting and relaxing was desperately needed in my busy world. I later had to get tested by the school district as a protocol to return back to campus for work; I tested negative. The modifications that COVID-19 forced me to make in my life were actually good. Adapting to new ways of doing things and looking at things through a different lens has been beneficial. A highlight of the COVID-19 pandemic was ministering to Mumbai, India via Zoom on Jacob's faith and perseverance. It amazed me to think that I didn't have to be physically present in India to make an impact.*[2]

Gemma Wenger, M.Ed, educator and author, founder of Gemma Wenger Ministries, Inc.

Charlene Eber

I have retired from producing film and television in Hollywood and moved to Palm Desert. There are a lot of homeless people here in the desert. In my former capacity as co-founder and secretary of World Alliance for Peace, I made certain that a homeless program was financially subsidized through the foundation. In the desert I took a hands on approach to the homeless. I befriended the homeless at church outreaches specifically designed to meet their needs. I showed love as well as prayed for them. During the lockdown churches are not open so it has been harder to continue outreaching with the homeless. We all need to

---

2. Gemma Wenger, interview by email, September 22, 2020.

Speak Up For Those Who Cannot Speak Up For Themselves

give what we can and pray for the homeless to be safe from exposure to the coronavirus.[3]

Charlene Eber, retired Hollywood Producer.

Olga Soler

I will never forget 2020 because it was the year of solitude and silence, when the unrelenting traffic came almost to a standstill and the hush allowed nature to breathe, as humanity, throughout the planet, hid from encroaching death. This was the year my darling granddaughter was born after her mother's 54 hour labor and we prayed for her into the world and I held her as she came forth bright eyed and full of wonder. It was also the year I could not hold her for long seasons because I was an essential employee in a rehab for homeless and addicted women and did not want to risk her to illness. It was a year of dependence on technology and of seeing the frailty of the same as computers brought us the power to create, and stay entertained, while informing us of its tragedies. It was the year I hated virtual life the most, missing eye to eye and skin to skin contact. I wrote plays and scripts and science fiction books and read till my eyes became dry and bleary. I took care of my sick husband and I rejoiced with him when he found his biological family online. I saw plays I could never afford on tiny screens instead of stage sets and sat pensive before movies I might never have seen. I saw people bursting with gratitude for what they usually took for granted. I saw families and friends long for each other and wish for a visit they used to make excuses to avoid. I redid artwork for books and sewed clothes. I edited my work till I hated it and loved it again. I grew a garden with wonderful vegetables and fourteen foot sunflowers. I gathered sticks and made a fairy house I wish I could live in. I saw my grandson play classical guitar self taught and my baby granddaughter learn to crawl on the tiny screen of my telephone. I encouraged women about to give up and saw others die because they did. I said goodbye to some people in disagreement

3. Charlene Eber, interview by text, September 15,2020.

> and some in death. I said hello to some who reached out in their own solitude. I got daily encouragement from believing friends over the phone. I prayed for everyone who came to my mind and for the tragedies of violence and fire and weather that were ravaging everywhere. I worshiped with people who wanted to worship online and stayed away from those who wanted to mix God with dirty politics. I struggled with my own sordid humanity and prayed for cleansing. I took pictures of odd things. I took long walks in unpeopled places. I cooked and shopped wearing a mask like a bandit. I got food and I shared it. I purged my house of the unessential. I ran through the whole gamut of my emotions from exhaustion to terror and back to acceptance and joy. I tried not to think about the darkness and decided to walk in the light. I prayed to see what God wanted me to see in all this and had to believe that despite the terrible disunity in the body of Christ and in this country, despite people still not understanding that Black lives need to matter too, despite bullies and overdoses and poverty amidst plenty, that prayers were being answered and were going to be answered and that God's will, would be done, despite us—on earth as it is in heaven.[4]

Olga Soler, performing artist, fine artist, author, educator, social worker.

Charlie Lehman

> God has been merciful to our family. We are all well. We are safely employed (with adjustments) or retired, so there is no change in our income. We are aware that so many others suffer, die, do without, and grieve. One person close to us has had COVID-19, and has recovered fully. We know that others suffer from fires, floods, storms, a huge explosion, homelessness, and displacement. Our church has adjusted, complied, and cut back. We continue to worship. My wife and I miss the usual contact with our brothers and sisters, and we are thankful for the contact we have. I serve at the altar when assigned. I do not volunteer. My

---

4. Olga Soler, interview by email, September 10, 2020.

wife attends services when scheduled. We missed watching our son run the Boston Marathon, and we had no summer vacation. Because I am triple-compromised, my wife does the shopping and picks up my medications. I mask up, take my (doctor's orders) walks, and avoid people. Sometimes I go to the Post Office. Going to Home Depot or a bookstore is a big deal, almost a date. We dined outdoors once. A tank of gas lasts weeks. We are not critical of California's precautionary measures. Since the pandemic started, my respect for Governor Newsom has gone way up. Our family recognizes the danger, and we comply. We are thankful for our current life. We can do this.[5]

Charlie Lehman, author of Serve the People.

Aaron Ezra Mann

A grateful Not hateful word of encouragement. I, for one, am delighted how God is revealing such great mercy, grace and wisdom to his people during this season. Praise His Holy Name! Advertisements abound, "Buy silver or even better buy gold for security!" My response, simply put, you want security, buy Jesus instead—He's the gold! Many have said, "we're all in this together." I must disagree. We may all be wearing masks and in home lockdown at this hour, but God is dealing with us individually. I've learned to stay close to Him, because as the evil rises, so will God's precious anointing. We will see many forms of evil unfold with our very eyes. God is using the outbreak of COVID-19 to sanctify us, preparing His people for a brighter future. And those who choose Him in this hour will be blessed mightily! Bear in mind He is not a punishing God, but a loving God. So be of good cheer and above all—no unbelief! As a final thought from 2 Chronicles 7:14, "If my people, who are called by my name, will humble themselves and pray and seek my face and turn from their wicked ways, then will I hear from Heaven and will forgive their sin and will heal their land."[6]

5. Charlie Lehman, interview by email, September 12, 2020.
6. Aaron Ezra Mann, interview by email, September 23, 2020.

The Commission

Aaron Ezra Mann, Academy Award Winning Hollywood Producer.

Wilma Faye Mathis

Blessings in the midst of Pandemic 2020 (COVID-19). During this time of the pandemic there were lessons learned and appreciation gained. My overall takeaway is, to do things differently is also to do things better. Health Improvements: Having to undergo a major surgery was a decision I put off for quite some time. Presumably, I was to be back on my feet within three months, but things didn't go quite as planned. Once I stopped viewing my recovery in a negative way and appreciated the fact I was still in good health, I took advantage of indoor opportunities to stay and get back on track. Exercise: In addition to rehabilitation therapy, I invested in a stationary bike to aid in my recovery process and to reduce stress. Recipe Book: Although I had plenty of books, this time I focused more on healthy meals, turned to protein shakes, and eating more fruits and vegetables. Resting: I am one who stayed on the go and rested when I can. Because going out was not an option except for a doctor's appointment and someone driving me around, I rested more. Taking time to think, focus, and to weigh what to put energy into and what to dismiss. Although not 100%, but on my way one day at a time. This particular journey is taking some work, but making small adjustments works best for me and I am okay with that. Social Life: You can call me an extrovert and actually I do not mind because I enjoy socializing with people whom I admire and we connect. However, I can be an introvert when I need to, usually as a result of me being occupied and needing to shut everything else out. I had to focus on me and not think it selfish for not being there for everyone demanding my time and attention. This season allowed me to become more at peace while introverting, and to appreciate the advantages this space had to offer. Keeping in touch: I reverted to what I used to do when I was younger. It may seem "ole school" today, but I decided to communicate again through mail. Yes, "snail mail," which may be foreign to some in this generation. While I am an advocate of email, text, messenger, etc., nothing in my opinion can replace the personal touch when someone goes out of their way to communicate. To do this meant searching for the appropriate card befitting for the individual, ordering, creating mailing labels, and purchasing stamps. This really brought me back to my younger days when I sat down excited to express myself in a letter, mail it to the person, and await their response. When I received the call or thank you note, it was such a good feeling and no matter what else was going on, I felt loved. This is what I experienced with sending cards and notes again to family, friends, loved ones, during this time in the pandemic. Sometimes it is the little things that make a difference: lifting someone's spirit, putting a smile on another's face, in small but meaningful ways. Family Time: This is the big one! Family has always been a primary focus of my life, and over these months of health recovery and the pandemic, my appreciation has deepened. Take, for example, family birthdays, holidays, and special celebrations. My family is known for big gatherings (and I mean big!). We are a large family, but have many friends and extended family members. Although the friends and extended family were missed during COVID-19, the intimate time with my immediate family was and remains priceless. Intimate Moments: I love to travel and will jump to every opportunity that comes my way. When you are always on the go, you miss things right in front of you. One of the things my niece and I started having was TV night. It started off watching our favorite nighttime soap operas. Yes, I watch them in between the Hallmark channel. Then it turned into regular movie nights, and times we would just "sit and chat," sometimes for hours. We would gather in the living room with popcorn and snacks and have the best time ever. As I started progressing in my health, my passion for cooking aroused. Being on the go, I ate on the go. My dad, who is my hero (my shero mom too) loves homemade chili. I'm talking about the kind that takes all day to make. Well, guess what, periodically I would let the family know in advance and spend the day in the kitchen making homemade chili. It became known as "family chili night" coupled with cornbread and my version of Arnold Palmer.

The Commission

Not sure if I ever shared this with my family, but these times helped me to realize that a situation I began viewing as negative, turned into a blessing and for that I am grateful! Mother and Son Bonding: My son who is now grown (still my baby) had plans to make moves in his life as most men who desire to do better and become self-sufficient. It turns out with the major surgery that I had, and after being hospitalized and in rehabilitation for almost a month, coming home required personal assistance. I knew my son was compassionate and would help in any way he could, but to see his demonstration of care for his mom gave me an even greater appreciation. You may wonder why? A New Appreciation: My son is an only child and I have done everything in my will for him. I have experienced sickness through the years, but none that left me incapacitated for more than a few days. But during this time I needed help in every way: getting in and out of bed, the shower, daily massages of my wounds, food preparation, getting dressed, going in and out of the house to appointments. Not only did he do these things, but I felt love and compassion speak through him saying, "now I get a chance to take care of my mom for all she has done for me." He is not one to talk a lot, neither will open up unless he is ready or you know how to pull it out of him. But the times we spent in conversation and he sharing his heart put me at ease that he was ready to be his own man and take on the world. I noticed this as I was recovering and able to do more for myself. He purchased a car and stepped out on his own. Most who know me thought, "how are you handling this?" Actually, I was content and it brought joy to me that even in the midst of a pandemic, family values remain intact and still growing. These memories are priceless! It's not Over: It is important that everyone knows themselves and does what makes them happy. What works for one may not work for another. Meanwhile, I am on my path to wholeness: physically, emotionally, spiritually. I am ready for this next chapter of life while expecting amazing![7]

Wilma Faye Mathis, Teaching Assistant CUME, GCTS.

---

7. Wilma Faye Mathis, interview by email, October 10, 2020.

LeaAnn Pendergrass

Faith Trumps Fear: When I sat down to eat a salad on March 10, 2020, the news was full of COVID-19 fear and it was starting to affect me. I heard the Lord speak so clearly to me as I sat to eat and I put down my salad and listened. Joshua 1:6–9: God guides Joshua: "Do not be afraid, do not be dismayed, I am with you wherever you go." And then God instructed that I post communion services daily on Facebook Live and share it publicly to bring peace to the world. This began my daily communion the next six months on Facebook which has reached a multitude of believers. In Isaiah 26:3, the prophet explains: "You will keep in perfect peace, those whose minds are steadfast, because they trust in you." I continued to share live ministry outreaches of the past six months: baptism on the beach, street ministry to Hollywood boulevard, tent revival meetings. These events empowered by the power of the Holy Spirit brought the lost to Jesus who were physically present and also those who viewed the Facebook posts. The miracle-working power of Jesus' shed blood on Calvary poured out over us during the pandemic. Praise the Lord, in the past six months the pandemic has become a wide open mission field.[8]

LeaAnn Pendergrass, Founder of My Gathering Place International.

Paul Jacobs

I started 2020 with great expectations to relax, travel and work part time as an environmental protection consultant. I retired at the end of 2019 after an approximately forty year career in environmental protection, specifically in air pollution control and climate change. In January 2020, I heard that a new virus was hitting the Wuhan region of China. Having traveled to China numerous times in my career on air pollution consulting missions, I have communications with folks there. I then heard about the early warnings being communicated to the residents of Chinatown,

---

8. Lea Ann Pendergrass, interview by text, September 23, 2020.

San Francisco, reminiscent of years earlier with H1N1. I watched the San Francisco government jump on the issue early on prompting quick action by Governor Newsom. I watched a public health issue become politicized resulting in further dividing the United States of America and causing needless COVID illnesses and deaths. Fast forward to today, we are approaching one million COVID-19 cases in the United States of America, have major civil unrest as racism still rages in America and, most recently, unprecedented heat waves (Los Angeles hitting 120 degrees) and wildfires raging the western region of the country resulting from climate change-induced droughts and severe heat waves. During all of this, two uncles passed away: Donald Thayer and Ralph Jacobs (also my godfather). My wife and I were exposed to COVID-19 at the funeral, were tested and thank God tested negative. Additionally, the economy has tanked, unemployment has skyrocketed, we are experiencing unprecedented levels of anxiety and other mental health issues as a result of COVID-19. Generally people are in a survival mode, scared, hungry for leadership and normalcy. I pray to Pope Francis and the good Lord daily that we will get back to normalcy and human decency soon. Our very survival depends on it.[9]

Paul E. Jacobs, environmental protection consultant.

Christopher Hodgkins

When David had angered the Lord with a warmongering census in 2 Samuel 24, God gave the King of Israel three unpalatable options: seven years of famine, three months of military defeat, or three days of deadly plague. David chose plague, for, he said, "let us fall now into the hand of the Lord, for his mercies are great; and let me not fall into the hand of man" (v. 14). My own experience during the worldwide COVID plague has confirmed the truth of David's terrible choice; I've fallen into God's hand, and I've seen grace upon grace. Most obviously, my immediate family and I—spread across eight time zones from

---

9. Paul Jacobs, interview by email, September 18, 2020.

Vancouver to Boulder to Houston to Greensboro to London—have been well, and indeed no one whom I know has yet died from the virus, with very few infected. But more importantly than a personal, 98.6 safety not experienced by some others, the dislocation and isolation worked by this plague on all of us have reaffirmed for me the home truth of Genesis that "it is not good that the man should be alone." However much some seek to portray social distancing as the "new normal," it is nothing better than a necessary evil, and may the handshakes, backslaps, embraces, and kisses return with great relief and relish sooner rather than later, gone with the suffocating anonymity of masks. The COVID time also has made me cherish our precious rights to freedom of assembly and worship, freedom of movement, and freedom of speech, as a plague of fear—warned against by leaders across the political spectrum at the COVID outbreak—has descended on our cities, towns, schools, churches, and families to drive us unnaturally apart and indoors, conditioning us to see our neighbor as an existential threat, and to silence dissenting ideas. Finally, Coronatime has dimmed the glamour of the virtual; all Zoomed out, we have never experienced the unfiltered and unmediated thingsomeness of the actual (an aroma, a mountain, a face-to-face classroom) as so glorious and gorgeous. May this plague bestow one more blessing before it departs: may it remind the earthling Adam in all of us that we were made for each other, and for that searing and saving meeting with our Maker, face-to-face. Then this time in God's hand will have reshaped us indeed.[10]

Christopher Hodgkins, PhD, educator and author.

Charles Hodgkins

Living someplace where the population is measured in tens of thousands rather than millions has its advantages once a worldwide health catastrophe starts to unfold. I punctuated my 2010s by trading one SF for another: in 2019, I moved from San Francisco to Santa Fe, where the

---

10. Chris Hodgkins, interview by email, September 13, 2020.

> *population is around 1% of the Bay Area. Little did I know the COVID pandemic would nearly knock our world off its axis months after I settled in northern New Mexico. My move has given me the open space I was looking for — not only in Santa Fe's high-desert landscape at the base of the Rockies, but also in my schedule and my life. Leaving the big city behind has allowed me to restructure my priorities the way I hoped. And ever since the pandemic came crashing in to offer all these extra at-home hours, my flexible work schedule has helped me make time to keep up with my dad and distant friends via more frequent video calls. I've also been able to hike more often than I ever did in California, pursue creative projects, explore my new home region, and simply lounge in my yard amid the perennial Southwest sunshine. The pandemic's been awful in so many ways. It's taken lives, it's crashed economies, it's forced us to cover our faces, it's bolstered our culture of fear. So it's no surprise that anxiety feels dangerously high these days, nationally and globally. And yet, on a personal level, that creeping anxiety feels manageable most of the time here in my underpopulated world at 7,000 feet. I'm grateful for this and a whole lot else.*[11]

Charles Hodgkins always wanted to work with his hands. But surgery seemed impractical and cobblery's heroic age had passed. So he turned to writing.

Jasmine Myers

> *God works in the weirdest of ways. When gatherings became unsafe in March, all of our scheduled Easter performances were cancelled, and when the lockdown hit in the middle of the month, it cancelled our plans to get together to film the show. Instead, we ended up shooting a version in which each actor shot his or her own pieces alone at home, which the director then cut together. (Providentially, it was a monologue-based show, so we could do this with only a small amount of rewriting.) Because it was filmed, the show ended up reaching more people than we ever*

---

11. Charles Hodgkins, interview by email, October 12, 2020.

would have reached in person, and because of the way it was filmed – highlighting the isolation of the characters – it spoke in a special way to those quarantining during the pandemic. We were even, by God's grace, able to get it dubbed into Farsi so that one of our ministry partners, Heart4Iran, could use it in their Gospel broadcasts into this closed but spiritually hungry country.

Postponing our summer show indefinitely (we're hoping to do it next summer) allowed us to take a much needed break from being in production mode all the time, as well as to do some actor training, which left us with some new friends and some training videos we'll be able to reuse in the future. We were also able to hold some worship times together as a company – a welcome time of being together as a community without the pressure of trying to get things done. Thanks to a forward-thinking board member, Still Small is now embarking on a new adventure of offering online performances, so that churches can hold contact-free events for their communities. We're starting with The Prophet Project, which was filmed in 2019, but we're hoping to add more and more of our shows. The online performance packages will also include access to a six-part video Bible study series, so that audiences will be able to delve deeper into the show and the God behind it. This is an answer to years of prayer, as we've sought ways to make the discipleship we do in rehearsal available to churches and audiences. It also will allow our non-touring shows to have a life beyond the end of their run – and is an answer to our prayers for God to expand our reach, as offering shows online effectively erases geographical limitations on "where" we can go. We don't know what else God wants to do, but we know He does all things well, and one thing we've learned over the years – both through repeating the Truth in our performances, and through experiencing His faithfulness in our many adventures and emergencies – is that He is absolutely trustworthy.[12]

Jasmine Myers, CEO and Founder of Still Small Theatre Inc.

---

12. Jasmine Myers, Interview by email, September 23, 2020.

Section Four

Words of encouragement from ministers to comfort and reassure us

Joanne Petronella

John 14:26:
"But when the father sends the Counselor as my representative—and by the Counselor, I mean the Holy Spirit—he will teach you all things and will remind you of everything I myself have told you" (NIV).

> The Greek word for "counselor" or "comforter" means "enabler," and the end result of the Holy Spirit's work in each Christian's life is deep and lasting peace that provides a confident assurance in any circumstance. I warn against the spirit of fear, emphasizing that true believers have no need to fear the present or the future. I explain that, while contemporary life is full of stress, Christians must allow the Holy Spirit to fill them with Christ's peace by praying to and worshiping Jesus and meditating on the Word of God.[1]

---

1. Joanne Petronella, DeFazio and Spencer, *Redeeming the Screens*, 140.

Joanne Petronella, founder of Christ In You The Hope Of Glory International Ministry.

Linda Lockhart

Go blow them horns cried Joshua, the battle is in my hands. These lyrics from the well known African American spiritual "Joshua Fought de Battle of Jericho" describes the epic Biblical account (Joshua 6:15–21). God speaks to Joshua telling him to march around Jericho for six days. On the seventh day, God tells Joshua to march around the city seven times while the priests blow their ram's horn trumpets. At the sound of the trumpets, Joshua told the people to shout. They shouted "with a great shout" (Joshua 6:20), the walls fell down, and Joshua's army won the battle.

God has called Linda to blow the shofar. She describes her experience blowing the shofar during the pandemic in a Christian service located in the Swedenborg Chapel on the Harvard University campus and in an outdoor service at the Veteran's Memorial Park in Beverly, Massachusetts. Amos 3:6 explains: *The shofar has the quality to stir the hearts and to inspire love, as it is written: "Shall a shofar be blown in a city and people not tremble?"*

> *The sound of the shofar traditionally calls the believer to repent and be proactive, not just pray. This is so important for the season we live in. Scripture commands that the shofar be blown to warn that the day of Jesus' return is near. (Joel 2:1: "Blow a trumpet in Zion; sound an alarm on my holy mountain! Let all the inhabitants of the land tremble, for the day of the Lord is coming; it is near.") I was glad to see that the response of the church communities to the shofar was very positive. As Psalm 89:15 explains: "How blessed are the people who know the joyful sound!" This joyful sound is the teruah (blast) of the shofar.*[2]

Linda Lockhart, former supervisor, Anchorage Home for Boys, Thorndike Street, Beverly, Massachusetts.

---

2. Linda Lockhart, interview by email, September 10, 2020.

April Shenandoah

> Lately, I have been thinking about the words of Proverbs 18:21: "Death and life are in the power of the tongue, and those who love it will eat its fruits" (NRSV). Our lives mirror what we speak, producing fruit after their own kind—be it rotten or sweet. The words we speak today will produce the life we live tomorrow. May our words be uplifting to others. Words are power in action and will either bless or curse. This message, if taken literally and practiced with perseverance, will bring victory over chaotic living and the challenges we face. . . . Take every opportunity to be a mouthpiece for Jesus. Time is short! Seek first the kingdom of God and his righteousness, and all these things shall be added to you (Matthew 6:33).[3]

April Shenandoah, author, Ambassador of Prayer.

Susan Stafford

Susan Stafford is a great relational evangelist. She reaches out with the love of Jesus to the up and out and the down and out. She tries to help everyone the Lord places in her path. *When I asked her to contribute to this dialogue, she kindly responded: Dear Jeanne, Thanks for thinking of me. I'm glad to share my thoughts with you as you continue to reach out to so many.*

> Satan would love to have us think that life is being taken from us. While COVID-19 continues to be a challenge, the key is when walking with the Lord Jesus Christ, you're exactly where you're supposed to be and nothing is wasted in His hands! My work as a Chaplain has been limited without being able to hold someone's hand while we pray or give them a needed hug. Due to the restrictions, I'm not able to visit patients in the hospital or nursing homes and it's very sad to see how alone they are without family or friends at their bedside. Weddings have been postponed and even funeral services are delayed so that's been quite discouraging on a human level. We are limited to Zoom

---

3. April Shenandoah, DeFazio and Spencer, *Redeeming the Screens*, 106.

at this point. The threat of our lives never being the same again can be devastating. And yet when the Lord is our focus, we understand why the martyrs who preceded us were able to remain strong. The Lord is in charge of our final journey and our trust is in Him.[4]

Chaplain Susan Stafford, Ph.D.

Bob Yerkes

Zechariah 4:6: "This is the word of the Lord unto Zerubbabel, saying, 'Not by might nor by power, but by my spirit.'"

> The purpose of this message from God to Zechariah was to encourage Joshua and Zerubbabel in their work of restoring the temple and the nation of Judah after the Babylonian captivity. They were shown that the true source of power was not merely by might, not by human power, but by the Holy Spirit's anointing. This vision assured Israel that, despite the hindrance of the work on the temple, Zerubbabel would finish it (Zech 4:8–10). Bob credits his spiritual and physical survival to his understanding of his vision to Zechariah: not by force, nor by strength, but by my Spirit. . . . Bob realizes that these keywords were highlighted for him by God's Spirit. Bob has come to realize that it is only through God's spirit that he has come to accomplish anything of true value. Zechariah 4:6 reminds Bob continually that he is on Jesus' side, and Bob has brought that message to many. . . . As he lived for God, Bob was determined not to trust only in his own strength or abilities but rather to depend on God. Bob has moved in the power of the Holy Spirit, becoming a well known witness for Jesus in the acrobatic stunt and entertainment industry. Bob Yerkes credits his spiritual and physical survival to his understanding of God's vision to Zachariah.[5]

Bob Yerkes, acrobat and Hollywood stuntman.

---

4. Susan Stafford, interview by email, September 14, 2020.
5. Bob Yerkes, DeFazio and Spencer, *Redeeming the Screens*, 55.

Speak Up For Those Who Cannot Speak Up For Themselves

Ted Baehr
The Movieguide® Experience During the Pandemic

Movieguide® has grown tremendously since March 2020 as a result of the various shutdowns, lockdowns and other interesting exercises of extra-constitutional acts by the state and federal governments. Since most people are staying home, their consumption of streaming, pay per view and any other forms of entertainment have increased dramatically.

So those who were concerned about choosing the good and rejecting the bad and helping their children to choose the right entertainment increased their use of Movieguide® in all of its formats. Within a year we went from 37 million to 41 million viewers in every area of our activities from television to radio to various different platforms on the internet. For instance, in a short period of time this spring, our Facebook viewership increased to 416%. Also, for the first time I filmed a short testimony for Movieguide® and as of this writing, well over a million people watched it, and then many made decisions for Christ. Of those who made professions of faith in Jesus Christ, ninety percent were men and sixty percent were men under twenty-four, which is interesting since I'm seventy-four years old. On a personal level, my focus has been primarily on my wife who has been on chemo drugs and infusions for twenty-four years and has had as of this writing a major six week operation and procedure in Houston for her eyes and a major operation at USC Keck Hospital to remove her uterus, bladder and other body parts. (They were looking to remove her heart, but I stole it years ago.) That said, people whom I know who are in the extremely vulnerable category for this minor pandemic, such as over eighty years old or suffering from bone marrow cancer, had insignificant cases of coronavirus COVID 19. As an attorney, who does not practice, I try to look at all the evidence, and as a former research engineer who worked with a company that tested and developed rocket fuel for NASA in the 1960s to get a rocket to the moon, I try to evaluate all the possibilities. The coronavirus COVID-19 is noteworthy, but certainly not on the level of the black plague, the bubonic plague *and other pandemics that have occurred in history. Even in those pandemics, faithful Christians went out of their way to take care of the suffering Christians, such as Martin Luther took people with the black plague into his home even when people told him not too. More recently Albert Schweitzer and Mother Theresa have exhibited Christian love in similar ways. So the pandemic has not been a threat in our lives except for the fact that it has caused a tremendous increase in government control by officials who ignore the law and do not evaluate all the scientific information and yet pretend to be influenced by both. The worst consequence has been the shutting down of churches and the reaction of many of us to allow this government overreach as if they were sheep led on the way to the slaughter. With that said, I understand the concerns and applaud everyone who's exercised discernment and wisdom, and who does not succumb to a theology of fear but who has remained confident that God is in control since He alone is omnipotent, omniscient and omnipresent. Satan is the harbinger of fear. The news media has succumbed to gaining viewers and listeners by constantly spreading fear, but the consequences of all this fear-mongering is like trying to fish by throwing dynamite into a pond; it destroys everything rather than save, rescue, or catch the few.*[6]

Ted Baehr, founder and chairman of The Christian Film & Television Commission™ and Publisher of MovieGuide®.

Pastor Bob Rieth

So many people are isolated during the pandemic. I appreciate Pastor Bob Rieth for allowing me to include his recent devotional on loneliness in this book! Loneliness is a disease of our time. Loneliness has nothing to do with the number of people in the room. In fact, we often feel more alone in a crowd. We are lonely when we have a hole in our heart that longs for companionship and understanding. We overcome loneliness when we have one or more relationships with people who care. Ultimately, we need

---

6. Ted Baehr, interview by email, September 16, 2020.

to turn to our Lord and Savior for companionship and comfort. He has promised to be with us 24/7. "On my bed I remember you; I think of you through the watches of the night. Because you are my help, I sing in the shadow of your wings. My soul clings to you; your right hand upholds me." Psalm 63:6–8. Still, we need the presence of another caring person to dispel our feelings of aloneness and sadness. "This is why I weep and my eyes overflow with tears. No one is near to comfort me, no one to restore my spirit." Lamentations 1:16. This works both ways. Sometimes we are the ones in need and sometimes we are the ones that God will use to give comfort to others. We do not need to be trained counselors in order to be a comforter. We just need to be willing to be used by God to reach out in Christian friendship to those around us. 1. Be Approachable. Does someone who is hurting feel free to tell us his or her problem or ask us for help? Do we change the subject, tell a joke, or quote a Bible verse? Are we willing to share their pain or do we offer a platitude? Or, even worse, do we start to tell them our own problems, past or present? 2. Be Available. Are we so busy with our own lives that we have no time to see those around us? It does take time to listen and reach out to help someone. At the end of the day, what will count the most? Beware of the barrenness of a busy life. 3. Bear one another's burdens. Sharing the pain of someone's burden divides the pain and multiplies the relief. Even though we may not be able to change the situation, we can let them know that we care and share their grief. "Carry each other's burdens, and in this way, you will fulfill the law of Christ." Galatians 6:2. Loneliness can trouble any of us. No one is immune.

Remember these three helpful thoughts: 1. Jesus cares and has promised to be with us always. Let the presence of Jesus wash over us and comfort us. When we are content, we can be alone without being lonely. 2. We can comfort those in any trouble with the comfort we ourselves have received from God. Paul stated this principle so clearly in 2 Corinthians: "Praise be to the God and Father of our Lord Jesus Christ, the Father of compassion and the God of all comfort, who comforts us in all our troubles, so that we can comfort those in any trouble with the comfort we ourselves have received from God. For just as the sufferings of Christ flow over into our lives, so also through Christ our comfort overflows." 2 Corinthians 1:3–5. We need to be receptive to the efforts of others to help us. Be willing to accept the words and gestures of friendship from others. This reminds me of a song we used to sing in Sunday School: "Jesus and Others and You." What a wonderful way to spell JOY. With love and care, Pastor Bob Rieth[7]

Pastor Bob Rieth, Founder of Media Fellowship International.

Mel Novak

Grace, mercy and peace from God the Father and from Jesus Christ, who is with us forever.(Matthew 28:20).We need to hold on to that promise during these dark days of the coronavirus worldwide lockdown. I pray that you all are protected with good health, virus free, praying on your "whole armor" as we are commanded in Ephesians 6:10–17. It is crucial to be "suited up and booted up" as they say in prisons. You must pray in faith, never doubting (James 1:6). Doubt leads to unbelief. You must pray with praise for the answer. I praise the Lord anyhow. Praise evicts the forces of darkness. Praise dispels doubt (Philippians 4:6, 7; Psalm 100:4) and brings healing. It is crucial for you and me to pray and praise. There is more in the Bible about praise than there is about prayer. Pray according to God's will. God answers prayer.[8]

Mel Novak, Actor, Skid Row and Prison Minister.

Bruce I. McDaniel

Staying Apart Together. It started as a news story about a mysterious new virus somewhere in China. Then came the news that people were getting sick and dying on the west

---

7. Bob Rieth interview by email, September 20.2020.
8. Mel Novak interview by email, September 15, 2020

coast. Then it reached the New York City area. And then it was spreading out of control—a pandemic.

And so began months of masks and hand sanitizer. I washed my hands more often and took my temperature in the morning. I tried to stay at least six feet away from other people.

I learned new phrases: "social distancing," "contact tracing," "shelter in place," "essential businesses," "flatten the curve." My church suspended services. "Non-essential" businesses were shut down. A week after my wife and I started wearing masks in the supermarket the governor ordered that everyone wear them in public. We entered a "new normal" of empty shelves in the supermarket where the toilet paper used to be. . . using credit cards instead of cash so nobody would have to touch money. . . curbside pickup for restaurant take-out orders. I drove my wife to and from work so she could avoid the bus. My hair grew too long as the barber shop waited for permission to re-open. The news was full of stories of people dying in isolation from their families or being unable to visit loved ones in nursing homes. People were losing their jobs and being threatened with eviction and loss of their businesses. The sickness and death and economic distress fell disproportionately on people of color, bringing long-existing inequities into sharper focus.

But there were also stories of heroism on the part of medical personnel and first responders.

A friend who knew that I was a veteran called to point out that the number of deaths from the pandemic had reached the number of American service members lost in the Vietnam War. As the months went by, the toll would grow far beyond that. My wife and I were fortunate. We both receive Social Security, so we still had income. I had a writing project to keep me busy at home. We live near a park where I could continue going for walks without getting near other people. But we are years beyond the cutoff for being considered "old people," and I was driving elderly people to the supermarket every week. We had to be careful not to get the virus and spread it to others. I found ways to be active in the church without being around people. Sunday morning meant watching my church's on-line *service on our computer. I learned how to use Zoom for church meetings and Bible Studies. Three times a week I put food in an outdoor "Blessing Box" at the church from which neighborhood people could take what they needed. The boxes of macaroni and cans of vegetables and the toilet paper that I put into the Blessing Box always disappeared, so I knew that someone needed them. After six months some restrictions had loosened up, but it was clear that the pandemic was nowhere near over. Although our country has a long history of individualism, it seemed to me that this was a time when we had to reach into our equally deep tradition of cooperation and community spirit—pulling together to do what was good for our country, even if it meant temporary sacrifice of some personal choices and convenience. This was a time that called for patriotism. If we could "stay apart together" I was confident that, with patience and God's help, we would get through this.*[9]

Bruce I. McDaniel lives in Rochester, New York, with his wife Thurma. A retired indexer of legal publications, Bruce spent time at home during the pandemic writing a science fiction story.

Valerie Crisman

One of the things God has really impressed on me during the COVID pandemic is how good it is to stand on His promises. Very early on, as the severity of the pandemic began to sink in, I realized what it meant to me that I have a sure and certain foundation in Jesus. Having lived through 9/11, I remember the first scripture that I heard at that time was Psalm 46, and its opening verses ring true to me in this season as well: "God is our refuge and strength, a very present help in trouble. Therefore, we will not fear, though the earth should change, though the mountains shake in the heart of the sea." As a pastor and as a Christian called to share my faith with others, I feel that this is the heart of the message God would have me share right now. God is dependable. God is trustworthy. God heals and protects. God saves. Because we can trust in Him, we

---

9. Bruce I. McDaniel, interview by email, September 29, 2020.

have nothing to fear. Of course, that doesn't mean that we don't take precautions to avoid getting sick, but it means that our life doesn't have to be overcome with worry.

Our church spent a few weeks meeting separately in our homes with worship materials I provided. Then we switched to Zoom, did a few outdoor services, and finally returned to our building with Zoom available for those who couldn't worship in person. We had a few members lose jobs and lose family members to COVID. We even had a member pass away, and we never were able to determine what happened to him or have a funeral for him. But no matter where we worship or what our circumstances during the pandemic, I always want people to hear this message: God can be trusted, and God is in control.[10]

Valerie Crisman, Pastor, Pilgrim Church

2020's challenges at times seemed beyond human strength and abilities but miraculously God provides strength to survive lockdown, grief due to loss of loved ones to the coronavirus, extreme weather patterns, wildfires, evacuation during the pandemic and racial violence. These authors spoke out of the love of Jesus in their hearts, standing on the belief that we *triumph over Satan by the blood of the Lamb and the word of our testimony* (Revelation 12:11). These authors reminded us that we are called to be a voice:

> We too are called to be voices, temporary voices which God will use to prepare the way in our generation. We are the voice for this time and for this place. Our role is temporary, but it is essential. Without the voice, people will not hear.[11]

This brief book is a prayer putting God in remembrance of the promises of His Word (Revelation 21: 3–6):

> "Look! God's dwelling place is now among the people, and he will dwell with them. They will be his people, and God himself will be with them and be their God. He will wipe every tear from their eyes. There will be no more death or

---

10. Valerie Crisman, interview by email, October 1, 2020.

11 Vryhof, "The Nativity of John the Baptist," Lines 228–235, accessed June 24, 2020.

> *mourning or crying or pain, for the old order of things has passed away." He who was seated on the throne said, "I am making everything new!" Then he said, "Write this down, for these words are trustworthy and true."*

The 2020 pandemic, wildfires and racial violence will not destroy us:

> *We will move past this because God has chosen us as his dwelling place. We can persevere, if only we remember who God most fundamentally calls us to be: ourselves, bearers of Christ in the world, not by virtue of particular accomplishments, but because of the love with which God has made us.*[12]

---

12. Lucas Hall, SSJE, "What is God's Call?"

Afterword

Martha Reyes

Lessons Learned

I am usually the teacher, but during this pandemic, I have allowed life to teach and test me in many ways. I have always said that *"worse than suffering* would be *suffering in vain."* Every trial is a stop sign in life. We can no longer continue to live on autopilot because now the safe pathway has been intercepted. Suddenly it is divided into two uncertain paths. Amid confusion, pain, or *shock*, we are supposed to make decisive and life-changing decisions. Really? There are no clear and specific traffic signals: it is up to us to discern or guess. If we choose well, we inventory reserves of goods, health, emotional and spiritual resources. By raising awareness of these resources within reach, we reposition ourselves, opt for positive change to move closer and closer to victorious endings and marvelous blessings.

But if we make the wrong decisions, there could be more pain, more losses, wear and tear, illness, or, in extreme cases, death.

As one human race, three great forces unite us: *a common lineage, a unifying project,* and a *fearful enemy.* In these times of pandemic, we have all three operating and interacting to twin us more than ever. In times like these, we should realize that we are not divided among tribes, parties, flags, races, but we are one humanity longing for the same solutions. We have been fixated for months now on "numbers" in the hope of transitioning to healing and transacting to a new reality with a sense of normalcy.

These are times of real confrontation with the "unpredictable."

We can no longer remain apathetic or indifferent. We need to activate spiritual gifts and reserves of intellectual abilities, sometimes silenced by personal distractions, confusion, anxieties, and fears. In difficult times we are called to navigate the deep wells of the subsoil of the soul to get out of the superfluous. The task at hand is to save ourselves from physical and psychological damage, and still have the strength to willingly protect others.

After this pandemic or after any tragedy, iconic images will be tattooed and immortalized in our memories for years to come.

This is my list of memorialized lessons:

- There are still a lot of good people in this world. The good is not only the holy, the psychologically healthy or virtuous, but also the person who intends to invest enormous efforts without expecting the usual rewards. We see this in health care professionals and first responders.

- Human beings do not change their behaviors easily with discourses, exhortations, resolutions, but with new inner virtues that spring forth, transforming their internal paradigms and essences.

- Losses arouse nostalgias. Suddenly, we begin to appreciate what we had abandoned or wasted by being ungrateful custodians of what we took for granted.

- Physical lockdowns silence loud external commotions, clearing unbearable noise levels. Now we can listen to inner voices that so often tried to speak to us with surprising eloquence and discernment.

- There is no substitute for simplicity that oxygenates the heart.

- Amazingly, we can live with less money, less fun, less hatred, less division, fewer wars, crimes, selfishness, violence; we were expert hoarders of all of these.

Afterword

- We need more of emotional connections, faith, hope, resilience, shared purpose, and collaboration.
- We cannot live without God, without prayer, without our spiritual quests and supernatural encounters.

We understand that our life before the pandemic was half-healthy and half-madness.

For too long we spent a lot of time trying to feed insatiable hearts that, by going after the superfluous and temporary, kept ignoring the superiority of truth. Being our lives indeed threatened in a way never experienced before, we come to the same conclusions: that the most pressing thing in life is *to live*, even a few more days. Someone fought once for our first heartbeat: now it is up to each one of us to fight for our last breath.

Let us stay calm. Stillness can still make room for the invisible motion of ideas and new purpose. We always try to dodge pain, but what a unique gift when we allow suffering to carve a better essence and a new "no nonsense reality." Mother nature and Father God are always trying to teach and correct if we could only listen.

About the Authors

Julia Davis ED.M from the Harvard Graduate School of Education, and an ED.M from Bouve College of Health Sciences at Northeastern University. She has held teaching certificates in New York, Massachusetts, and the District of Columbia and has been certified as an Assistant Principal and as an Assistant Special Education Supervisor. Julia has taught in the public and private sector in community-based programs including METCO, Summer STEP opportunities for underrepresented populations in science and technology and Head Start. She has served as a member of Parent's Advocacy Group for Massachusetts supporting FAPE and mainstreaming Special Education students. She has taught pre-K through all 12 grades, Adult Non- Readers, Limited English Language Learner's and GED Preparation courses. Julia taught internationally as an undergraduate exchange student in a Special Education Program based in Newnham on Severn, Gloucestershire, England, which operated under the auspices of Antioch College in Ohio. Julia and her husband Dan have three children and three grandchildren. They attend the International Family Church in North Reading, Massachusetts. Julia developed a monthly prayer breakfast program for the Everett, MA community.[1]

Jeanne DeFazio is a SAG/AFTRA (Screen Actors Guild – American Federation of Television and Radio Artists) actress of Spanish-Italian descent, who played supporting parts in theater, movies,

---

1. DeFazio and Spencer, *Empowering English Language Learners*, 150–151.

About the Authors

and television series, then served the marginalized in the drama of real life. She became a teacher of second language-learner children in the barrios of San Diego. She completed a BA in history at the University of California, Davis, MAR in theology at Gordon-Conwell Theological Seminary, and a Cal State Teach English Language Learners program. From 2009 to the present, she has served as an Athanasian Teaching Scholar at Gordon-Conwell's multicultural Boston Center for Urban Ministerial Education. She is the co-editor of Creative Ways to Build Christian Community, Redeeming the Screens, Berkeley Street Theatre, and Empowering English Language Learners. She co-authored with Teresa Flowers: How to Have an Attitude of Gratitude on the Night Shift and edited Keeping the Dream Alive: A Reflection on the Art of Harriet Lorence Nesbitt and Specialist Fourth Class John Joseph DeFazio: Advocating for Disabled American Veterans. [2]

Martha Reyes was born in Puerto Rico and has resided in California, ministering to Hispanics in the United States and internationally since 1978. She has traveled to more than twenty-two Latin American countries and many parts of Europe and the Middle East, giving concerts and retreats on inner healing and participating as a guest speaker in national and international conventions on healing and restoration. From 1992 until the year 2000 she organized the acclaimed Hosanna Multi-Festivals conventions, international events with representatives from thirty countries in music, theater, and arts, held annually in Mexico, Florida, and Israel.[3]

---

2. Spencer and Spencer, *Christian Egalitarian Leadership*, xi.
3. DeFazio and Spencer, *Redeeming the Screens*, 90–91.

Bibliography

Almquist, Curtis, SSJE. "Making Meaning." Cowley. Volume 47, Number 1, Cambridge: 2020.https://issuu.com/ssje/docs/2020_cowley_fall___pages.

"Arts Health and Well-Being." The Welsh NHS Confederation.May 2018. https://www.nhsconfed.org/-/media/Confederation/Files/Wales-Confed/Literature-review-of-arts-and—health-and-wellbeing.pdf.

Boud, David. "What is Peer Learning and Why is It Important?" https://docs.google.com/document/d/1gvu5_yZTvgnxWCfD_rovhcFKLKm8jBLxqDj7gegee34/edit.

DeFazio, Jeanne and John P. Lathrop, eds. *Creative Ways to Build Christian Community*. Eugene: Wipf and Stock, 2013.

DeFazio, Jeanne and William David Spencer, eds. *Empowering English Language Learners*. Eugene: Wipf and Stock, 2018.

DeFazio, Jeanne. *Keeping The Dream Alive*. Eugene: Wipf and Stock, 2019.

DeFazio, Jeanne and William David Spencer. eds. *Redeeming the Screens*. Eugene: Wipf and Stock, 2016.

Khalil, Ashraf."During the pandemic,D.C. volunteers provide food for the needy." PBS. April 9, 2020. https://www.pbs.org/newshour/health/during-pandemic-dc-volunteers-provide-food-for-the-needy.

Everett, Burgess. "Senators Duel Over Race Card." Politico. 5.23.14. https://www.politico.com/story/2014/05/jay-rockefeller-john-johnson-race-106983.

Flowers, Teresa and Jeanne DeFazio. *How to Have an Attitude of Gratitude on the Night Shift*. Eugene, OR. Resource. 2014.

Laurence, Kenneth. and Keleher, Terry. "Structural Racism." For the Race and Public Policy Conference 2004. https://www.racialequitytools.org/resourcefiles/Definitions-of%20Racism.pdf.

Lucas Hall,SSJE,"What is God's Call?" Cowley. Volume 47, Number 1, Cambridge: 2020.https://issuu.com/ssje/docs/2020_cowley_fall___pages.

"Life, Liberty and the Pursuit of Happiness." https://en.wikipedia.org/wiki/Life,_Liberty_and_the_pursuit_of_Happiness.

Martin Luther King, Jr."I Have A Dream Speech" Wikipedia. https://en.m.wikipedia.org/wiki/I_Have_a_Dream.

Bibliography

Nagourney, Adam."Jerry Brown on a California Exodus:"Tell Me Where Are We To Go?" *New York Times*. 9/14/20. https://www.nytimes.com/2020/09/14/us/politics/jerry-brown-on-a-california-exodus-tell-me-where-are-you-going-to-go.html.

Spencer, Aida B. and William D. Spencer, eds. *Christian Egalitarian Leadership: Empowering the Whole Church According to the Scriptures*. Eugene: Wipf and Stock, 2020.

Spencer, Aida B. and William D. Spencer. "Applying Biblical Truths Today. 'Responding to Floyd Killing: Creating Action Teams As Safeguards.'" June 8,2020.https://aandwspencer.blogspot.com/2020/06/responding-to-floyd-killing-creating.html.

Spencer, Aida B. and William D. Spencer. "Applying Biblical Truths Today. 'Who's Fault is the Virus?'" April 8, 2020.https://aandwspencer.blogspot.com/.

Vryhof, David. SSJE. "The Nativity of John the Baptist." June 25, 2013.https://www.ssje.org/2013/06/25/the-nativity-of-john-the-baptist-br-david-vryhof/.

"We Shall Overcome." http://blogs.christianpost.com/scriptural-truths/we-shall- overcome- 177918/14. Sept. 2013.

www.ingramcontent.com/pod-product-compliance
Lightning Source LLC
Chambersburg PA
CBHW070101100426
42743CB00012B/2629